# SEW Sentimental

**Easy Scrapbooking Techniques**

Linda Lum DeBono

# Martingale®
& COMPANY

Sew Sentimental: Easy Scrapbooking Techniques
© 2007 by Linda Lum DeBono

Martingale & Company
20205 144th Ave. NE
Woodinville, WA 98072-8478 USA
www.martingale-pub.com

## Credits

President & CEO: Tom Wierzbicki

Publisher: Jane Hamada

Editorial Director: Mary V. Green

Managing Editor: Tina Cook

Technical Editor: Dawn Anderson

Copy Editor: Candie Frankel

Design Director: Stan Green

Assistant Design Director: Regina Girard

Illustrator: Adrienne Smitke

Cover Designer: Shelly Garrison

Text Designers: Shelly Garrison & Stan Green

Photographer: Brent Kane

Printed in China

12 11 10 09 08 07        8 7 6 5 4 3 2 1

**Library of Congress Cataloging-in-Publication Data**
Library of Congress Control Number: 2007028390

ISBN: 978-1-56477-775-1

## Mission Statement

Dedicated to providing quality products and service to inspire creativity.

## Dedication

To the many individuals who have inspired me on this journey.

**For Reno**
My rock. Thanks for keeping things going while I am plugging away at my work.

**For Adam and Alex**
My muses. Keep up the crazy antics, which inspire and entertain me daily.

**For my grandmothers, Irene and Yuet Yau, and my parents, Glen and Sally**
My foundation. Thank you.

**For my sister, Betty**
My sounding board. You are irreplaceable and talented.

**For my brother, Robert**
My loyal supporter. I am in awe of your talents too.

## Acknowledgments

Thanks to the following people who inspire me and give generously:

Tina Cook, Karen Soltys, Mary Green, and Dawn Anderson

Betty, Chun, and Jack Kwan

Garland, Jennifer, Emily, and Ellen Wong

Serena, Norm, Taylor, and Ryan DaPonte

Stephanie, Tony, Jared, and Ethan Leite

Mary Tan

Peter Kao

Angelo, Dorothy, Alyssa, and Daniel DeBono

Neal Caldwell, Karen Tallarom, and Emily Caldwell

Colleen, John, and Jane Gregory

Umashankau Sathya, Roopashri Melkote, and Abhay Bhatt

Jonathan and Maria Maddocks

For providing products for use in this book, I would like to thank the following companies:

Free Spirit Fabric (fabric), www.freespiritfabric.com

Printed Treasures (inkjet fabric sheets), www.printedtreasures.com

Warm Company (Steam-A-Seam 2), www.warmcompany.com

Ba Ba,
Your curiosity, passion, and unique vision continue to inspire me every day.
Love always, Oon Ding

# CONTENTS

Introduction  5

Tools of the Trade  6

Picture This: Notes on Photography  8

What's Your Style?  9

Stitches  10

Patchwork  18

Appliqué  22

Tags  26

Printing on Fabric  30

Words and Letters  34

Ribbons and Trims  37

Unique Ideas for Fabric  42

Embellishments  52

Borders  58

Pockets and Envelopes  61

Vinyl and Transparencies  64

Project Instructions  68

Product Credits  72

Patterns  77

About the Author  80

# INTRODUCTION

I have been documenting and journaling all my life, although my endeavors were never defined by any particular art form. Most of my "memories" were contained in a box, a diary, a photo album, or a blank sketchbook. I would happily scribble notes and adhere magazine pictures or paraphernalia, such as concert tickets and funky business cards collected on my journeys, in my notebooks. Nothing, however, resembled the sophisticated scrapbook pages that you see in magazines today. In my quilting, I also relied on words, and it was natural that words became an integral part of my quilting design process. When I started quilting, I would begin with a word and let myself be inspired by images conjured from that word. My design ideas would flow from what the word meant to me.

After I had my first son, Adam, I started scrapbooking a bit more seriously. It then seemed an easy progression to marry the two art forms, quilting and scrapbooking. My goal is to inspire you to create classic and simple memory projects that incorporate sewing techniques.

First, you will be introduced to the necessary tools and learn how to use them to produce great projects to preserve your cherished memories. Then you will be provided with some tips on style and photography to make your project stand out.

Subsequent chapters will guide you through all of the techniques that reflect the marriage of quilting and scrapbooking to make something new. They range from adding stitches to a scrapbook page to making your own fabric for quilting projects.

Throughout the book, easy techniques will be presented along with beautiful and simple designs to make for yourself or for gifts.

The key is to step outside the box and try new applications of old techniques. Something that seems old hat in sewing can result in a fun effect in paper arts. Most of all, enjoy making something that you and your family will cherish.

All the best,

Linda

# TOOLS OF THE TRADE

Good basic tools are essential to making your design process easier.

## Camera

A good basic camera, whether digital or film, is a necessity. Take it with you everywhere you go so that you can get candid shots of your everyday life. To take a great photograph, you don't need the most complex camera. All you need are a few clever tips and lots of practice. See "Picture This: Notes on Photography" on page 8 for tips on improving your photography skills.

## Computer and Graphics Software

Computer software programs are very useful tools in my design process. I use the photo editing software Adobe Photoshop and the illustration software CorelDRAW for most of my artwork. These powerful software tools allow me the flexibility to adjust and alter my photos, journaling, and artwork. I also like to draw my scrapbook layouts onto CorelDRAW to better visualize the sizes of the elements required.

There are simpler programs such as Adobe Photoshop Elements if you only need basic cropping and alteration operations, and any word processing program is perfectly fine for typing out text.

## Inkjet Printers and Inkjet Printable Fabric and Transfer Sheets

If you're printing your own photographs, then a great inkjet printer and specialty photo inks are necessary for good clear images. Printing personalized images on inkjet fabrics and on iron-on transfers gives projects a soft, handmade feeling. When printing on these products, be sure to use standard inkjet inks and not specialty photo inks for clearest results. Inkjet fabric sheets are paper-backed fabrics that are designed to be fed through inkjet printers. After the desired design, photo, or text is printed onto the fabric sheet, the paper backing is removed, leaving just the printed design on the fabric. For an example of this technique, see "How to Make a Pillow Accent from a Printed Fabric Sheet" on page 31. Inkjet iron-on transfer sheets allow you to print a design onto the transfer sheet, cut it out, and then fuse it onto a fabric. The "Keepsake Shoe Bag" on page 32 features this technique.

## Cutting Tools

**Craft knife and paper trimmer.** I use my craft knife and paper trimmer for cutting paper. The knife is ideal for cutting smaller, detailed images. The paper trimmer is used to cut larger papers with straight edges.

**Rotary cutter and self-healing cutting mat.** The rotary cutter is the standard tool for cutting fabric. A good self-healing cutting mat underneath is essential.

**Scissors for paper and fabric.** Use two separate pairs of scissors, one for cutting paper and one for cutting fabric. Two pairs are necessary to keep the scissors sharp. I also have a separate pair of Teflon-coated scissors for cutting fusible web.

## Adhesives

Many types of craft adhesives are available on the market, and most have overlapping purposes. Paper glue prevents curling and leaves the paper wrinkle-free when dry. Fabric glue dries very clear and is permanent. Over time and through experimentation, you will come to favor those products that suit your needs.

**Mounting squares and glue dots.** There are many different brands, sizes, and varieties of mounting squares and glue dots, and in the end it will be a matter of personal preference and intended use that determines which product to use.

**Fusible web.** Fusible web is used to adhere fabrics together and is especially good for appliqué projects.

**Liquid glues and sealers.** Yes! paste is a nontoxic, acid-free, nonrunning, noncurling glue that can be used to adhere paper, fabric, and other materials.

## Sewing Machine and Thread

A basic sewing machine capable of a straight stitch and a zigzag stitch is all that is necessary for adding stitches to scrapbook layouts. However, if you have more stitches on your machine, you can experiment and have more fun with your designs.

There are many threads available on the market today. I use regular cotton quilting thread for most machine stitching. Six-strand embroidery floss is ideal for handwork; I normally use three strands in my projects. Experiment with different weights and types of thread for handwork.

## Fabrics and Ribbons

**Fabric.** Any type of fabric can be used in your projects. The choice depends upon the desired mood, texture, and feeling that you are trying to convey. Fabrics that work well include cotton quilting fabric and canvas.

**Ribbons and trim.** Sold by the yard or in a variety package of precut yardages, ribbons in every color, pattern, material, and width are available on the market today to coordinate with your project. Ribbons are great for "sewing." Try making satin stitches and simple flowers.

## Papers and Papercrafting Supplies

**Paper.** A variety of papers, including cardstock, textured papers, patterned papers, and fabric paper, add interest to scrapbook pages and other projects.

**Scrapbooking embellishments.** To add texture and contrast to your work, choose from numerous scrapbooking embellishments, including paper flowers, woven labels, crystals, brads, alphabet stickers, grommets, buttons, clips, photo corners, and more.

**Papercrafting supplies.** A bone folder for scoring paper, markers for journaling, and punches for making holes or decorative corners are just a few of the little tools that you can add to your supplies list. These items can make the design process a little easier and more creative for you.

# PICTURE THIS: NOTES ON PHOTOGRAPHY

I always get asked, "What kind of camera do you have? It takes great pictures." I always tell them that it's not the camera; it's the photographer who's doing all the work!

I own two digital cameras—a Leica Digilux I and a Panasonic Lumix DMC-Z8. Before I caught the digital bug, I owned a Canon point-and-shoot model and a Nikon SLR. I still love taking pictures with these cameras, but the digital format offers me greater flexibility and instant gratification.

Let me get back to the original point. It is not the camera that makes great photographs. It is the work of the photographer. That's you and me. I have taken many photos over the years (over 16,000 digital shots alone) and the old adage is true: Practice makes perfect. Well, at least it gets you more consistent shots.

First, remember that the most important thing is to preserve the memory the best way that you can. Don't feel intimidated if the shots aren't great. Just document it anyway. Second, try the few simple tips listed here and keep practicing. Third, if you have some not-so-great shots, don't despair! With a little work, you can greatly improve your shots.

## Go Ahead, Take a Better Shot

**Get closer, they don't bite!** Take a closer photo of your subject by zooming in. Be honest, do you have a lot of shots where the person in the photograph is the size of a small dog standing on your front lawn?

Train yourself to compose your shot through the lens. There will be less editing later.

**Use the rule of thirds to compose a better shot.** The rule of thirds works like this:

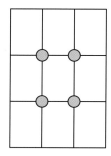

⬤ = Intersecting areas where you should strive to place your subject matter for the best results.

Divide the photograph with two vertical and two horizontal imaginary lines, spacing the lines equally apart. Photograph the subject by composing the shot so that the intended subject falls at one of the intersecting points.

**Turn off your flash.** Sure, sometimes your flash is necessary, but try taking a shot without it. Indirect natural window light is the best light to use for great indoor shots. When you are outside, overcast days are ideal for shooting good photos. If you need more light, try using a white board as a reflector. Any flat white surface can be used.

**Try a different angle.** Take a photograph from above or below a subject. You'll have more variety and an interesting perspective.

## Ways to Improve a Digital Shot

- Crop the photograph tightly while you are taking the photo and then edit with computer software if necessary. Consider changing the orientation of the photograph, that is, portrait or landscape, when editing.
- Delete busy backgrounds in your photograph with your photo editing software and replace them with a solid black color. See "Be Merry" on page 37.
- Cover an offending area by adding text, either with your photo editing software or by hand doodling.
- Turn the color photo into a black-and-white or sepia-toned photograph with your editing software.

## Ways to Improve a Photo from Film

- Compose the photo as best as you can while you're taking the photo.
- Have your local photo developer crop the photograph for you.
- Scan the photo into your computer and treat the new photo as you would a digital photo.

# WHAT'S YOUR STYLE?

I love simple graphic lines and saturated colors. If you want to be specific, I love chocolate, chartreuse, aqua, and fuchsia. I also love black-and-white photos with a photojournalistic touch. On my scrapbooking pages, I like to use a single large photograph rather than many small ones because I don't like a lot of visual distraction. I like the photograph and the journaling to tell the story. I take many photographs and don't have the space to frame them all. Since I keep a separate diary for my notes, I primarily scrapbook to highlight my favorite photographs.

With that said, I also don't limit myself to these criteria. They just give me a place to start. My taste in things is constantly evolving. I am influenced by everything around me. Magazines, fashion, blogs, books, home décor, and everyday things such as nature all have an impact on what I see when I design.

Start by defining your favorite things. It doesn't matter whether you are drawn to graphic or intricate lines, or saturated or muted colors. What are your favorite colors? Next define the project mood and topic. You don't have to stick to this plan exactly. I change my mind many times as I am designing because I often find that in order to make something fit into the whole picture, I have to tweak something else. Styles change and are flexible. Scrapbooking is a wonderful platform for exploring new applications because the projects require less time and investment than a large sewing project.

Look around you to see what inspires you and then add your personal touch through texture, pattern, color, or a technique that you favor. We all have our own style. Just let loose and express yourself.

# STITCHES

Stitching can be used to construct a project, but it can also be used as an accent. Whether done by machine or by hand, stitches can add texture and color to a project.

I Am

Who I Am

**Mother**, wife, daughter, sister, friend.

What I Am

Caring, **honest**, generous.

Why I Am

Visual, passionate, **artistic**, daring

How I Am

Artist, **designer**, business woman, author.

I am proud of who I am.

**That's me.**

## Me

Sew a grid on a piece of cardstock. Print journaling text onto another piece of cardstock. Trim to size and punch curves at the corners of the cardstock pieces and the photograph, using a corner rounder punch tool. Staple a woven label to the journaling block and adhere alphabet stickers to it. Mount the photograph and the journaling block on the cardstock. Attach flowers with a brad. Adhere a knotted ribbon and a metal tab with the year to the layout.

# Machine Stitches

When I first learned how to quilt, I was afraid of ruining my quilt. It took me a long time to quilt that first quilt. After that I was hooked.

I hesitated briefly when I first put stitches on my papercrafts, but I told myself that I could easily make another project. Give yourself permission to go for it and add some stitches to your projects! Mistakes can be fun, especially if you are adding free-motion stitches (see "How to Free-Motion Stitch" on page 12).

Start with a grid to add some texture to the background of your project. As you gain confidence, pull out your free-motion foot and cut loose by sewing some wavy stitches, circles, or your own designs.

Add some free-form frames around photographs, or decorate rubber-stamped images with stitches. Use machine stitched lines as a journaling guide.

For those of you with a lot of different stitches on your machine, try out a stitch that you may never have considered for your sewing projects because it just wasn't you. Sometimes stitches used on a smaller scale make a visual impact that may not have been possible on a larger sewing project.

If you are still not convinced that you can accomplish the machine stitching by yourself, go to a fabric shop and look for fabrics that have stitching as part of the design.

## HOW TO STITCH A GRID

1. Lightly draw grid lines the desired width apart onto cardstock.

2. Stitch on the marked lines in one direction. Turn the cardstock and stitch on the marked lines in the remaining direction.

## Summer Fun

Position a photograph onto cardstock, stitch a frame around it, and trim to size. Mount the photograph onto coordinating cardstock and trim ¼" around it. Cut patterned paper with pinking shears and stitch it to the background cardstock. Stitch about ½" away from the edges of the background cardstock. Adhere alphabet stickers, a flower, and the photograph to the background.

## HOW TO MAKE A STITCHED FRAME

1. Adhere a photograph onto cardstock and lightly draw a frame around it, about ¼" from the edges.

2. Sew around the photograph as many times as desired, using the marked lines as a guide.

## Thank You

Stamp flower images with acrylic paint in a random pattern onto cardstock. Machine stitch around the stamped images several times as desired, using free-motion stitching. Trim the cardstock and fold to make a card. Add an adhesive crystal to the center of each flower. Attach a woven label.

### HOW TO FREE-MOTION STITCH

1. Attach a free-motion or darning foot to your sewing machine and lower the feed dogs.

2. Set the stitch length to 0. Place the fabric or paper under the needle, lower the foot, and begin stitching. Use your hands to guide the paper or fabric under the needle following the desired design. Do not turn or rotate the fabric or paper under the needle.

## Love U

Sew patterned paper to cardstock. Arrange three photographs and a piece of cardstock for the journaling block into a 2 × 2 block for the center. Round off the four outside corners of the assembled block using a corner rounder punch tool. Sew guidelines on the journaling block and adhere text and a painted chipboard alphabet letter to it. Adhere the photographs and the journaling block to the background and stitch a line across each rounded corner. Attach a photo turn at the center.

## Emily at 4

Cut a scalloped edge on patterned paper and adhere to a cardstock background. Fold down the top edge of the cardstock, making a 5/8" flap. Sew a line of decorative stitches down the center of the flap through all layers. Adhere a photograph, a crystal alphabet sticker, and a text block to the background. Insert ribbons through a buckle and adhere to the card.

## Cool

Lightly draw circles onto cardstock with a pencil and then machine stitch on the marked lines. Mount a photograph to another piece of cardstock and mount a text block onto coordinating papers. Stitch around the text block. Adhere the photograph, text block, and three acrylic embellishments to the background. Apply the alphabet rub-on.

I see so much hope in this photograph of my Mom.
It shows me a young woman with so much ahead
of her.
Before moving to Canada.
Before marriage.
Before kids.
Before a career.

It shows me the woman before she became my Mom.

## Hope

Sew a piece of fabric to a cardstock background (the fabric used here has stitching as part of the design). Distress the edges of a photograph with ink, mount it to cardstock, and trim to create a border. Adhere the photograph to the background. Adhere a fabric embellishment and alphabet stickers to the background. Distress the edges of a text block with ink and adhere to the layout. Attach a brad at the corner of the photo through all layers.

Rub a brown, black, or sepia tone rubber stamping ink pad at an angle along the edges of papers and photos for a distressed look.

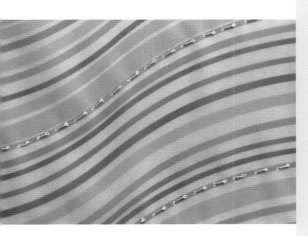

# Hand Stitches

I enjoy handwork, but I don't always have the time to do it. I found that sewing a small hand-stitched detail to a scrapbooking project or greeting card is the perfect way to resolve my problem.

Embroidery stitches such as lazy daisy, French knot, chain stitch, satin stitch, and cross-stitch are some of the easiest hand stitches and embellishments that you can add to your projects. They're quick to do and add so much elegance.

You can use a chain stitch to stitch a letter to a project or to sew a flower. Use thread, ribbons, wool, or whatever fibers you want to create unique effects. With the variety of products on the market today, the possibilities are endless.

## EMBROIDERY STITCHES

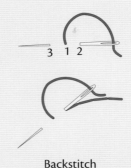

Backstitch

Blanket stitch

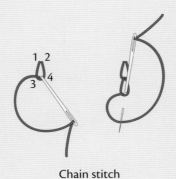

Chain stitch

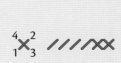

Cross-stitch

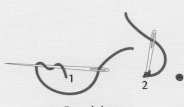

French knot

Lazy daisy stitch

Running stitch

Satin stitch

first ride

First ride.

We hadn't purchased a bicycle for you yet so you borrowed our neighbor's. Off you went, around and around the playground with Alex helping you along the way. You had tons of fun and were so excited that you could actually ride a bicycle! It seemed like only yesterday that you were a baby just starting to walk and here you are taking off on a bicycle almost by yourself! Ride on, the future is right ahead of you.

August 2006

## First Ride

Print text onto cardstock and adhere photographs to the page. Punch holes and tie ribbons along the right edge of the cardstock. Add rub-ons to the page and backstitch the arrow using three strands of embroidery floss (see "Embroidery Stitches" on page 15).

## Snow

Adhere and stitch fabric paper and cardstock to a piece of background cardstock. Adhere photographs and title letters to the background. Hand embroider cross-stitches around the letters for the title using decorative thread (see "Embroidery Stitches"). Stitch acrylic snowflake embellishments to the layout with machine satin stitches at the centers.

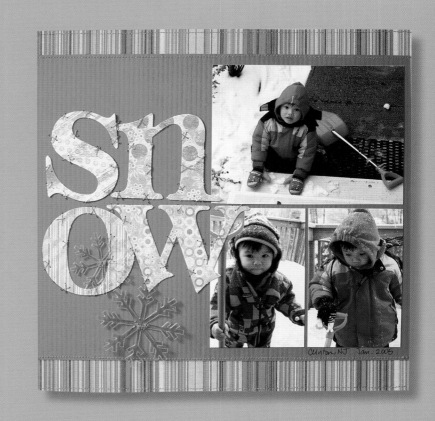

you love to jump in the puddle just outside our front door. ✱

I love to see your excitement over the ordinary things like puddles + rain. Aug 06

## Rain

Machine stitch patterned paper to a background cardstock. Adhere a photograph, machine stitch around the photograph, and adhere alphabet stickers to the page. Write text and hand sew a running stitch following the pattern on the paper (see "Embroidery Stitches"). Repeat as desired.

**RAIN**

# PATCHWORK

Traditionally, a patchwork design is created by stitching individual pieces of fabric together to create a larger design. Adding fabric patchwork to a paper project gives your project a handmade feeling. You will find instructions in this chapter for creating a simple Nine Patch block. Use a perfectly pieced block or, for a funkier look, a very crooked piece.

You can also make paper patchwork designs by stitching pieces of paper together. I love paper! I have lots of it and can't think of a better way to show it off than to piece together a fun background for scrapbook pages.

## Daniel

Create a paper patchwork on a cardstock background. Stitch around the edges of the patchwork pieces. I used a zigzag stitch here. Straight stitch ¼" from the edges of the background. Distress the edges of three photographs with ink (see "How to Distress with Ink" on page 15) and adhere the photographs and chipboard alphabet stickers to the stitched background. Staple ribbons in place. Attach a photo turn with a brad.

# Paper Patchwork

I just hate to throw my paper scraps away. I found that patchwork provides the perfect opportunity to use my scraps.

The easiest way to pull together several papers in a design is to purchase a line of coordinating papers. All you have to do is select your favorites from the group and you're on your way to a great layout.

I usually start with the photograph. Then I can size the photograph to the scale of the pieced background and the patterned papers.

Paper patchwork does not require adding a seam allowance. Just butt the pieces up to each other and stitch over the butted edges.

Or, to add dimension to paper patchwork, add seam allowances to the paper pieces and join the papers creating an exposed seam on the right side of the patchwork.

## ← HOW TO CREATE A PAPER PATCHWORK

1.  Sketch a layout of your design, including the dimensions of the patchwork blocks.

2.  Cut out block shapes from paper to correspond to your sketch. Adhere the paper blocks to a cardstock background.

3.  Stitch over the butted edges of the papers with a zigzag or decorative machine stitch. Or, if desired, stitch over the edges of the papers with hand stitches, such as cross-stitches (see "Embroidery Stitches" on page 15).

## Friend

Stitch three strips of paper together with exposed vertical seams. Distress the edges of the seam allowances with ink (see "How to Distress with Ink" on page 15). Trim the pieced paper to size and stitch it to the background cardstock. Mount a photograph onto another piece of cardstock, trim to create a border, and adhere it to the page along with fabric alphabet stickers.

## HOW TO CREATE AN EXPOSED SEAM

1.  Add a ¼" seam allowance to the edges of the patchwork pieces where the exposed seam is desired.

2.  Sew the pieces wrong sides together. Open out the pieces and finger-press the seam allowances open.

HAPPY HOLIDAYS! YOU ARE SO
ADORABLE IN YOUR SANTA'S
HELPER HAT. I KNOW THAT
SANTA WILL BRING YOU LOTS
OF TOYS BECAUSE YOU'VE BEEN
A GOOD LITTLE BABY!!

DECEMBER 2003

Ho Ho Ho

## Ho Ho Ho
## Holiday Patchwork Pillow

For a personalized gift, make this adorable patchwork pillow
using your favorite photograph and a special holiday message.
Project instructions are provided on page 68.

Ho Ho Ho

# Fabric Patchwork

Here's where things get easy for all of us fabric lovers!

Pull out your fabric stash and add a delicate touch to your paper crafting projects! With all the different styles, colors, and patterns of fabric available today, it is easy to find something to match the mood of your photograph. If you have an unfinished quilting project, perhaps this is the perfect place to show off some of what you started.

## Love

Trim a piece of cardstock to 10" square and sew to a cardstock background. Roughly sew nine 2" to 3" squares together to create a Nine Patch block. Sew the block to the background. Adhere a photograph to the block and arrange lengths of ribbon around the edges; at each corner, crisscross the ribbon ends and secure with a brad. Adhere a fabric embellishment and metal alphabet letters to the layout.

## HOW TO MAKE A NINE PATCH BLOCK

1. Cut nine squares from fabric, adding ¼" seam allowances as necessary.

2. Sew two squares right sides together, using a ¼" seam allowance. Sew a third square to the pieced unit to form the first row. Repeat to make two more rows. Press the seam allowances to one side.

Make 3.

3. Sew the rows together and press the seam allowances to one side to complete the block.

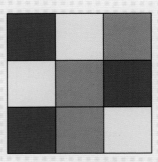

Nine Patch block

# APPLIQUÉ

In my quilting designs, my signature technique is appliqué. I love to appliqué words onto my designs, but appliqué can also include shapes and images. You can use the same techniques to add some whimsy to your scrapbooking projects.

## Appliqué Images from Paper

**H**

Adhere a photograph, a text block, and two patterned papers to a background cardstock, creating a patchwork design. Cut a letter appliqué from fabric paper, using a cardstock letter as a template, and adhere it to the layout. Zigzag stitch around each patchwork block and the letter appliqué as shown.

### USING COMPUTER FONTS AS APPLIQUÉ IMAGES

Print the desired style and size of a font on printer paper. Cut out the letter or number. Using the cutout as a template, trace the letter or number onto the desired art paper. Cut out this shape and adhere it to your layout. Embellish the letter or number with stitches as desired.

You love to switch the first letter of certain words with the letter H. It is so cute but we try to gently remind you of the proper pronunciation.

**Helephant = elephant**
**Halmart = Wal-mart**
**Hoysaurs = dinosaurs**

September 2005

### HOW TO MAKE PAPER APPLIQUÉS

1. Draw the desired image onto paper and cut out. No seam allowances are necessary.

2. Adhere the cutout to the desired project or background paper.

3. Decorate the cutout if desired by stitching around the edges.

## Little Pink Purse Card

Fold a piece of cardstock in half. Draw a purse shape with handles onto the cardstock, placing the base of the purse on the fold line. Cut out the purse shape through both layers. Use the cardstock shape as a template to cut a second purse shape from fabric paper, eliminating the purse handles. Adhere the two pieces together and fold in half.

## Appliqué Images from Fabric

### Blue

Cut a piece of cardstock slightly smaller than the front of a blank card. Machine stitch horizontal lines randomly on the surface. Cut freehand flower shapes from felt. Adhere the flower appliqués and stitch over the petals as desired. Adhere a crystal in the center of each flower. Trim the side edges of the cardstock with pinking shears. Adhere the decorated cardstock to the card front.

### HOW TO MAKE FUSIBLE FABRIC APPLIQUÉS

1. Trace a reversed template onto the paper side of fusible web, following the manufacturer's directions.

2. Cut out the image just outside the marked line and fuse to the wrong side of a scrap of fabric.

3. Cut on the marked line, remove the paper backing, turn right side up, and fuse.

4. Decorate the appliqué with stitching, if desired. If the appliqué was fused to a fabric background, place a piece of stabilizer under the project in the area of the appliqué before stitching. Remove the stabilizer after stitching.

## Independence

Cut title lettering and bracket appliqués from the desired fabrics. Adhere three photographs to a cardstock background and fuse the appliqué letters and brackets in place. Stamp the word *Independence* with ink and write the text. Machine satin stitch the corners of each photograph in place and stitch around the edges of the page.

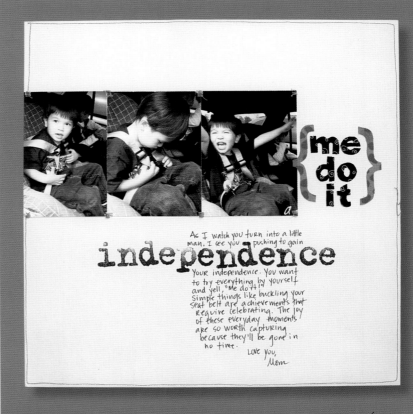

# VROOM

## Vroom

Cut letters from felt and zigzag stitch them to a background cardstock. Adhere patterned paper and a border strip to the background. Create a text block and trim the corners with a corner-rounder punch tool. Adhere the text block to cardstock and trim to create a border. Adhere the text block and photographs to the page. Embellish with fabric tabs and an alphabet sticker. Stitch around the edges of the page.

## Bloom Wall Hanging

Make this pretty quilt with floral and letter appliqués for that special little girl in your life.
She'll adore the perky colors and the bright flowers. Project instructions are provided on page 68.

# TAGS

Use paper and fabric tags to experiment with a technique that you may be hesitant to try. It is easy to try out something on a smaller scale before attempting the same technique on a large project. I love to test different color combinations on little tags. They're fun and easy to make.

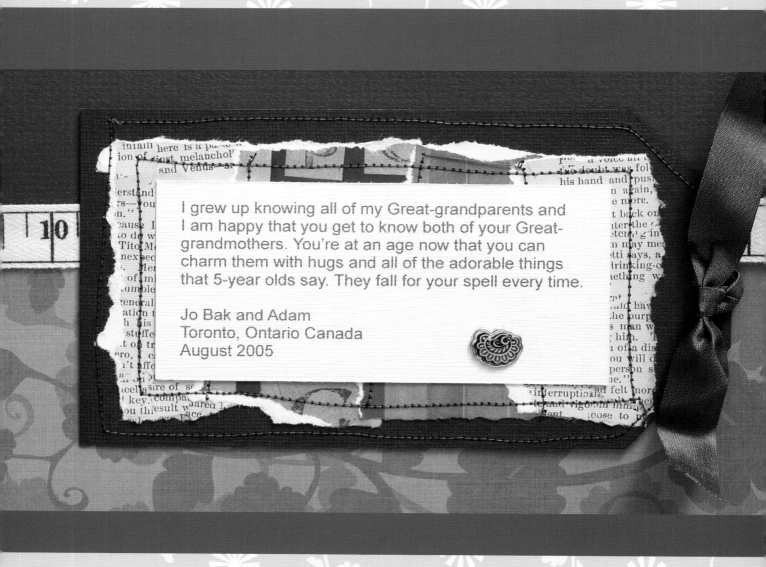

I grew up knowing all of my Great-grandparents and I am happy that you get to know both of your Great-grandmothers. You're at an age now that you can charm them with hugs and all of the adorable things that 5-year olds say. They fall for your spell every time.

Jo Bak and Adam
Toronto, Ontario Canada
August 2005

## Tags Made from Paper

Paper tags are great for decorating presents and showcasing snippets of information on scrapbooking pages.

For a quick present, cut out some identical tags, decorate them, and then sew them together to form a booklet.

## Paper Tag

Cut a shape from two different pieces of card-stock, using the pattern on page 78 if desired. Layer the papers with wrong sides together and edges aligned, and stitch ⅛" from the edges all around. Punch a hole at one end and tie a ribbon through the hole.

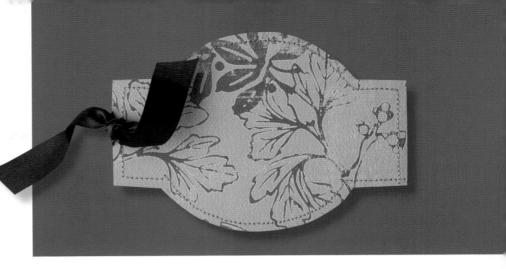

## Hugs

Adhere a border of patterned paper and a ribbon to a cardstock background. Mount a photograph onto corrugated cardboard, trim to create a border, and adhere to the page. Tear pieces of patterned paper and stitch them to a piece of cardstock cut into a tag shape. Adhere a text block over the torn papers and attach a ribbon and a brad to the tag. Adhere the tag and alphabet stickers to the layout.

### HOW TO MAKE A PAPER TAG

1. To make a tag, draw or trace the desired shape onto cardstock and cut out (use one of the patterns on page 78 if desired).

2. Decorate the tag with piecing, appliqué, stitches, or any other preferred method.

3. Punch a hole at one or both ends and tie a ribbon through each hole.

I grew up knowing all of my Great-grandparents and I am happy that you get to know both of your Great-grandmothers. You're at an age now that you can charm them with hugs and all of the adorable things that 5-year olds say. They fall for your spell every time.

Jo Bak and Adam
Toronto, Ontario Canada
August 2005

## Change of a Dress

Print text onto cardstock and then cut into a tag shape. Cut a dress appliqué from fabric and fuse to the tag (see "How to Make Fusible Fabric Appliqués" on page 23). Adhere a woven label to the tag.

## Tags Made from Fabric

Fabric tags add softness to a project. Be creative and incorporate images printed on inkjet fabric sheets into your fabric tags. These tags make wonderful gift tags for baby shower presents.

The most basic way to make a fabric tag is to cut the tag shape from a heavyweight fabric like canvas and decorate it. Otherwise, follow the directions below for lighter-weight fabrics.

### Fabric Tag

Make a template using the pattern on page 78. Cut tag shapes from heavyweight double-sided fusible stabilizer and two pieces of fabric. Fuse the fabric shapes to both sides of the stabilizer. Zigzag stitch around the edges and add a ribbon tie.

Mommy and Daddy welcome, with love

**Adam Lum-DeBono**

August 19, 2001
7 lbs. 13 ounces
21 inches

### Baby Tag

Cut out a tag from cardstock, using the pattern on page 78. Print an image onto an inkjet fabric sheet and pad it to make a pillow accent (see "How to Make a Pillow Accent from a Printed Fabric Sheet" on page 31). Stitch a journaling block to the tag. Adhere the pillow accent and alphabet stickers to the tag. Punch a hole in the tag and tie a ribbon through the hole.

### HOW TO MAKE A FABRIC TAG

1. Design your own tag shape or use one of the tag patterns on page 78. Draw or trace the shape onto the wrong side of the tag front and tag back fabrics and onto a piece of heavyweight double-sided fusible stabilizer. Cut out the tag shapes.

2. Fuse a fabric shape to each side of the stabilizer. Trim the edges even, if necessary.

3. Zigzag stitch around the outside edge of the fused layers and sew a ribbon to one end of the tag.

## Get Closer

Adhere two photographs and two pieces of patterned paper to a cardstock background to create a patchwork design. Zigzag stitch over the butted edges and straight stitch around the outer edges. Adhere lace and a chipboard letter to a fabric tag and tie ribbon at one end. Adhere a text block, alphabet stickers, and the fabric tag to the background. Attach flowers and ribbon borders with brads. Attach a small photograph.

Come on Adam, get a little closer to Jo Bak please. You're a cautious guy and this situation is no exception. You don't get to see your Great-grandmother often but you do love to visit … eventually. One of us, in this case, Daddy, is standing to one side of you trying to nudge you a little closer. It takes you a little while to warm up and then you're right in there helping her open her raffle tickets and playing with her. It just makes her day!

Great-grandmother Irene and Adam
Pembroke, Ontario Canada

August 2006

# PRINTING ON FABRIC

You can print your own photos and text onto inkjet fabric sheets to incorporate them into your designs. And you can create iron-on transfers with your own images to fuse to the fabric of your choice. There are also some preprinted fabric products available on the market, such as themed collections of images and words that can be cut apart.

Make sweet little keepsakes by printing out a photograph and then framing it or sewing up a little pillow. I made little keepsake bags for my kids' favorite baby things by taking photographs of the shoes or clothes, printing the photographs onto iron-on transfer sheets and then ironing the transfers to the front of muslin sacks.

Personalized printed fabrics are great for birth announcements too. It is a clever way to present the first photos of your precious baby. Just print the photograph onto a fabric sheet, stitch it to some cardstock, and decorate as desired.

### Alex Sweet Baby

Adhere patterned paper to a cardstock background and adhere ribbon over the edges of the patterned paper. Make a padded pillow accent from text printed onto an inkjet fabric sheet. Adhere a photograph to the layout and then adhere the pillow accent in place.

## Holiday Ornament

Print a photograph onto an inkjet fabric sheet and make a circular pillow accent. Punch a hole at the top of the pillow accent and tie a ribbon through it. Stitch a fabric square to the front of a blank card and adhere the ornament to the fabric square.

1. Print a photograph or text onto an inkjet fabric sheet following the manufacturer's directions. Layer the fabric sheet over a piece of thin batting and stitch around the outside of the photo or text block.

2. Use pinking shears to trim around the photo or text block, close to the stitching.

## Miracle

Distress the edges of a piece of patterned paper with ink (see "How to Distress with Ink" on page 15). Adhere the patterned paper to a cardstock background and staple the ribbons in place. Tie ribbons to a chipboard frame and adhere a patterned envelope to the layout. Adhere a ribbon around one short side of the frame, adhere the frame to the layout and secure the opposite end of the ribbon to the back of the page. Adhere alphabet stickers and words. Print a photo with text onto an inkjet fabric sheet (see "How to Print Photos with Text onto Inkjet Fabric Sheets and Iron-On Transfer Paper" on page 32) and make a pillow accent from it. Adhere the pillow accent to the layout. Adhere label stickers to the page.

## Keepsake Shoe Bag

Transfer a photograph of the actual baby shoes to a muslin sack to create this precious keepsake bag. Project instructions are provided on page 69.

Project instructions are provided on page 69.

first sneakers

## HOW TO PRINT PHOTOS WITH TEXT ONTO INKJET FABRIC SHEETS AND IRON-ON TRANSFER PAPER

I use the latest version of Adobe Photoshop, a professional photo-imaging computer software program, for my graphic work. I prefer to work in layers to ensure that the image or previous work on a project is left undisturbed while I compose the text.

1. Open your photo file and add a second layer by clicking on "Layers." Select "new" and then "layer" from the menu bar.

2. Select the text button and type the text. Adjust the font sizes, color, or opacity. Repeat the process to create additional layers of text if desired.

3. Print the photo with text onto a fabric sheet following the manufacturer's directions. Presto! You've got a great accent for your project.

## Jack

Print a photograph onto an inkjet fabric sheet. Cut out the photo, leaving a ½" fabric allowance all around. Tie ribbons around the frame. Cut a piece of batting the same size as the frame backing. Layer the frame backing with the piece of batting and the printed photograph. Wrap and adhere the edges of the fabric photograph to the back of the frame backing and then assemble the pieces in the frame.

# WORDS AND LETTERS

I love words and letters. I have them on almost every quilt that I have designed and on almost every project that I have made. I think that words and letters add a sense of funkiness to my designs. They offer a great way to inject some personality into an otherwise simple, yet effective, project. Use a much-loved computer font or simply draw your own letters for even more fun.

## Bébé You're Mine Wall Hanging

This is an adorable gift to make for that modern mom-to-be who has everything. It is a funky and decorative piece that makes a statement in any cool kid's nursery. Project instructions are provided on page 69.

## Name Pillow

This pillow project is a great present for anyone who wants to add a personal touch to his or her room. The large letters and bright colors will add a touch of whimsy to any space. Project instructions are provided on page 70.

## Initial Frieze

Make a monogram frieze as a gift for family or friends. A frieze is a fun and quick way to decorate the room of your favorite little one. You can easily match colors to a child's bedroom by choosing specific paint and fabrics for the project. Project instructions are provided on page 70.

## Fabric Letters

You can cut out your own fabric letters or use a set of precut alphabet letters on your designs for added texture.

### HOW TO CREATE FABRIC LETTERS

1. Roughly cut letters from fabric for the words you have chosen.

2. Adhere the letters to the project with a small amount of fabric glue and let dry. For a fun effect, do not completely glue down the edges.

3. Decorate the letters as desired.

## Love Greeting Card

Adhere pieces of ribbon to the front of a blank card to spell out the word *LOVE*, leaving a space for the *O*. Glue a flower in the reserved space and add a crystal to the center.

## Fishing

Adhere photographs and a strip of fabric paper to a cardstock background. Adhere fabric letters to the fabric paper. Attach a text block to the fabric paper with brads. Adhere letters and machine stitch in place. Machine stitch around the outer edges of the cardstock, the fabric paper, and the photo block. Apply rub-on alphabet letters.

THE CATCH

FISHING

You breathe it, you're obsessed with it. You have been fishing all of your life. My first memories of you fishing are the trips with Jo Gaun. I think that every kid loves to go fishing with his Grandfather.

Now that you live in Vancouver, you are into the serious stuff. You love the gear, the adventure, the comaraderie with Pete and you love the catch.

So cool.

September 2006

ROB

# RIBBONS AND TRIMS

Ribbons have many uses on scrapbook pages and add a splash of fun to any project.
Tie ribbons into knots or bows or use them flat to create stripes or borders.

## Ribbon Ties

Tying ribbons to a project is one of the easiest ways to add dimension to your work. Use round hole punches for a simple effect and tie one or more ribbons in each hole punched. For variety, try hole punches in different shapes and sizes.

## Be Merry

Fold cardstock in half. Punch holes near the fold. Score the card front near the fold, centering the holes, and tie ribbons through the holes. Add text to a photograph and adhere the photograph to patterned paper. Trim around the edges of the photograph with pinking shears to create a border. Adhere the photograph to the card.

## Tying Ribbon around Grommets

Grommets come in a variety of colors and sizes. Attach grommets near the edge of a page and tie ribbons through them to add color and texture to a layout.

**L**

Decorate a purchased wooden alphabet letter by tying several ribbons to it.

### Brother and Sister

Daniel, you have your Mommy's looks and are a charming and affable young man. I would go as far as calling you Mr. Personality because you love to chat with anyone who is willing to listen. You love anything related to the military and are a history buff.

Alyssa, you have definitely inherited Daddy's genes. You are a smart, shy, and articulate young girl. You love to sit for long periods of time and work on something crafty. You are good at reading already and you love all things related to ponies.

It is interesting to see the differences between brother and sister.

Daniel, 6 and Alyssa, 5

January 2007

## Brother and Sister

Punch holes in a piece of cardstock and attach grommets. Tie ribbons through the grommets. Sew a piece of patterned paper to the cardstock and adhere a photograph and a text block. Stitch around the text block. Stitch buttons to the layout.

# Ribbon Wraps

Wrap ribbon or trim around a photograph or any other element in your design to add a little sophistication. Trims with sequins will add some shimmer and sheer ribbon adds a subtle touch. The choices vary greatly—you'll have fun trying to pick the right accent for your project. All you have to do is wrap the trim or ribbon around the design element such as a photograph and adhere it to the back. I usually tape down the edges to prevent the ribbon or trim from fraying. For a more daring look, staple the ribbon to the edges of the project.

## Sweet

Round the corners of a square of cardstock with a corner rounder punch tool. Place small photos into a plastic sleeve and adhere to the cardstock. Adhere a large photograph to the cardstock. Attach flowers with brads and add a rub-on letter. Wrap bead and sequin trim around the photo block. Trim a piece of floral patterned paper, rounding the corners, and stitch it to a cardstock background. Stitch the photo block to the background on three sides, leaving the right edge unstitched. Make a paper tag (see "How to Make a Paper Tag" on page 27) and adhere it to the page. Adhere letter tiles to the layout.

## Clips

Your stationery shop is a great place to discover novel clips for attaching a ribbon, photograph, or design element to your project. You'll find your traditional paper clips and funkier, oddly shaped clips. Anything goes!

## Super Star

Round the corners of a piece of cardstock with a corner rounder punch tool. Layer and adhere a piece of patterned paper, the cardstock with rounded corners, the photograph, and a fabric sticker onto a cardstock background. Adhere journaling strips to the layout. Clip a ribbon to one edge of the layout and adhere the other end to the back of the page.

## Buckles

A buckle adds a tailored, sophisticated look to a design. It can be a shiny crystal-encrusted buckle for a high-fashion look or a wooden buckle for a more earthy feeling. Your local crafts shop or the notions department of your local fabric shop should carry a variety of buckles to suit your design requirements.

## Alyssa

Adhere a photograph to a printed background paper, adding photo corners on the top corners. Stamp an image on the right side of the photo and adhere alphabet stickers to the page. Adhere one end of a strip of fabric to the back of the page, pleat the strip across the front of the page, and insert the end through a buckle. Adhere the buckle to the page and sew through the middle of the fabric strip, up to the buckle.

# Ribbon Backgrounds

Add some ribbon in the background. You can space the ribbons apart, as I have done in "Emily's Holiday," or you can place the ribbons closer together or even weave ribbons together for a different effect. Try using different widths, textures, and colors for a mismatched look.

## Emily's Holiday

Stitch a piece of patterned paper and a piece of linen to a cardstock background. Adhere several ribbons across the linen, knotting each ribbon at one end and stitching the remaining ends in place. Adhere a photograph to patterned paper and trim to create a border. Adhere the photograph and a painted chipboard alphabet letter with journaling to the layout. Sew two rows of wavy stitching around three edges of the cardstock.

## Sweet Sachet

This sweet-smelling little gift is so quick and easy to make. Best of all, you can use up a lot of little pieces of ribbon from your stash. Project instructions are provided on page 70.

# UNIQUE IDEAS FOR FABRIC

Fabric elements make great accents for projects. Fabrics can be bleached, tucked, or stamped to make creative backgrounds. They can also be torn into strips, cut into photo corners, or stitched into yo-yo flowers to add interesting details to scrapbook pages. The possibilities are endless.

**E**
Tie-dye a piece of fabric with a bleach pen. Stitch patterned paper and the fabric to a cardstock background. Stamp images on the fabric with craft paint. Adhere a photograph, alphabet sticker, and crystals to the page. Secure the text block in place.

## Manipulating Fabric

There are many pretty ways to manipulate your fabric. One of the techniques I like to use is to create pin tucks. Just remember to start with a larger piece of fabric because it will shrink in size.

### HOW TO MAKE PIN TUCKS

1. Fold the fabric, wrong sides together. Stitch a scant ⅛" from the fold line.

2. Repeat step 1, spacing the tucks as desired.

3. Press the tucks in one direction.

### Fall

Sew pin tucks in a piece of fabric. Sew a patterned paper onto a cardstock background and then adhere the pin-tucked fabric and a photograph. Sew random zigzag stitches around the photograph. Stamp the title with acrylic paint.

## Bleaching Fabric

Bleaching your fabric gives some interesting effects and can add a very retro, hip element to your project.

### HOW TO BLEACH FABRIC

1. Cover your work surface with plastic and then bleach the fabric in one of two ways:

   • Draw or write on the fabric with a bleach pen, for very defined designs.

   • Tie the fabric with string in various places and paint the fabric with a bleach pen, for a tie-dyed effect.

2. Let the fabric dry and then rinse and press.

# Designing Your Own Fabric

Sometimes you can't find a coordinating fabric for your project. What are you to do? Design your own of course!

There are many ways to design your own fabric. You can start by drawing a design on the computer and then printing it out onto a fabric sheet. Or you can hand draw an object, scan it, rearrange it to your liking, and then print it onto a fabric sheet. I like to journal on fabric, too. Whatever the method, designing your own fabric is a really great way to personalize your project.

## HOW TO DESIGN YOUR OWN FABRIC

1. Draw a design or write text in a drawing program such as CorelDRAW or Adobe Illustrator. You can start from scratch or use one of the software tools, such as the brush, freehand, pen, rectangle, circle, or star tools.

2. Add color to the design as desired.

3. Print the design or text onto an inkjet fabric sheet.

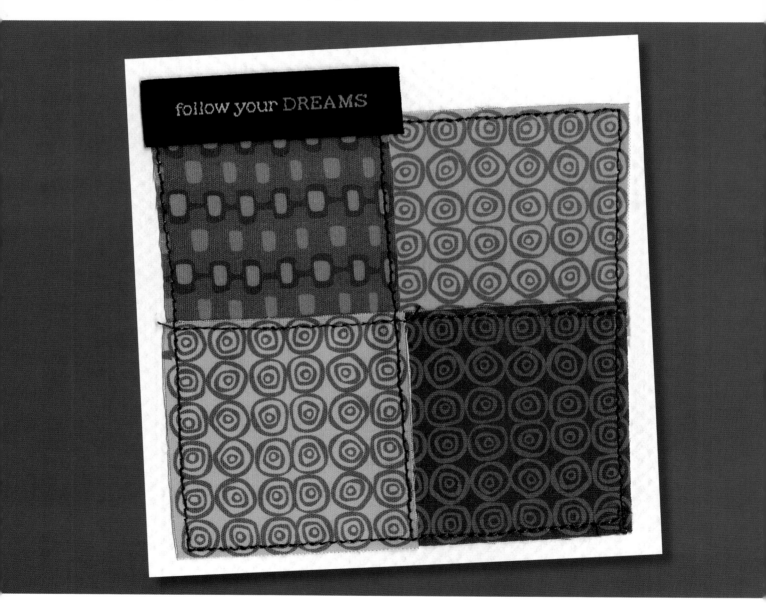

## Follow Your Dreams

Create a design for the fabric using an illustration computer software program. The images on these fabrics were created with a Bezier tool in CorelDRAW. Add colors to the created image and print onto an inkjet fabric sheet. Create four fabric squares. Sew the four fabric squares together to create a Four Patch block and adhere to the front of a blank card. Stitch around the outer edges of the patchwork block. Adhere a woven label to the card.

Metro Toronto Zoo, July 2006

## Explore

Print the desired text onto an inkjet fabric sheet and trim to size.
Adhere the fabric and several photographs to a cardstock background.
Stitch around the block of photos and around the fabric, close to the
edges. Add a rub-on title and journaling.

## Fabric Frames

For a tailored look, add a fabric frame around a photograph. You can cut a traditional frame that is an inch or two in width all the way around or design a frame with sides of varying widths so the photograph is off center.

### HOW TO MAKE A FABRIC FRAME FOR A SCRAPBOOK PAGE

1. Draw a frame pattern on paper, including an opening of the desired size. Allow extra space around the photograph to create an inner border, if desired.

2. Trace the reverse frame pattern onto the wrong side of fabric paper and cut out.

## Fabric Photo Corners

Fabric photo corners are a fun way to add a little spunk to your designs. You can tailor the look of the corners to any project by varying your fabric and color choices.

### HOW TO MAKE A FABRIC PHOTO CORNER

1. Trace the corner pattern and cut it out to make a template.

2. Use the template to cut the corner shape from the desired fabric.

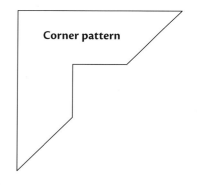

**Corner pattern**

I watched you sitting there silently looking out of the window of the train. You normally don't sit still for more than a minute and here you were all calm and quiet. I wondered what you were thinking about. What did you think about the throngs of people waiting to get onto the next train? Were you amazed to see all of the horse and buggies as our train steamed into the countryside? Or were you wondering when we would be pulling into the next station? You didn't say but you did sit there all intense and silent for a good five minutes. A rare moment indeed.

June 2006

## Intense

Make a frame and sew it to a cardstock background. Adhere a photograph to another piece of cardstock and trim to create a border. Adhere the bordered photograph, the text block, and alphabet stickers to the layout. Machine stitch around the corners of the text block.

1. Draw a right-angle triangle with two equal sides onto cardstock.

2. Draw a smaller triangle within the larger one. The size of the small triangle will determine the width of the photo corner sides.

3. Cut out the larger triangle. Cut away and discard the smaller triangle, leaving the template.

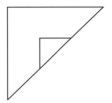
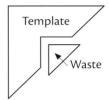

Template

Waste

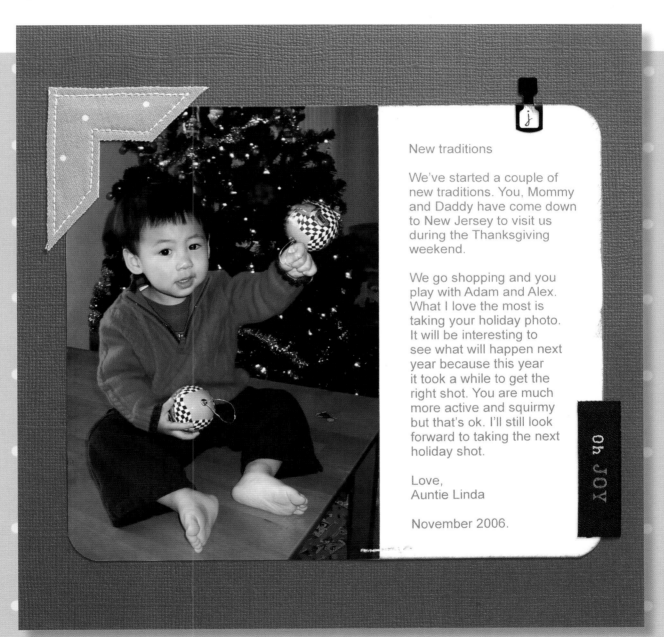

New traditions

We've started a couple of new traditions. You, Mommy and Daddy have come down to New Jersey to visit us during the Thanksgiving weekend.

We go shopping and you play with Adam and Alex. What I love the most is taking your holiday photo. It will be interesting to see what will happen next year because this year it took a while to get the right shot. You are much more active and squirmy but that's ok. I'll still look forward to taking the next holiday shot.

Love,
Auntie Linda

November 2006.

## New Traditions

Round two corners of a text block and the bottom-left corner of the photograph using a corner rounder punch tool. Distress the edges of the text block and the photograph with ink (see "How to Distress with Ink" on page 15). Adhere the text block, the photograph, and a woven label to a cardstock background. Add stitching as desired. Make a fabric photo corner and stitch it in place. Add a clip.

## Fabric Strips

Fabric strips add a lot of softness and texture to scrapbook pages. It is easy to mix and match different strips to make a coordinating collage for your background. To tear fabric strips, clip the fabric along one edge using scissors. Grasp the fabric on each side of the clip and pull in opposite directions to tear the fabric along the grain.

### Curly Qs

Tear fabric strips and layer and adhere them to a cardstock background. Stitch around the fabric block. Attach a photograph to the page. Add a metal letter with a brad to a corner of the photograph. Zigzag stitch around the photograph and straight stitch around the edges of the background cardstock. Add a fabric tab to the page. Stamp the title with acrylic paint and add journaling.

## Stamping Fabric

For some projects I like the subtlety of plain textured fabrics. Such is the case for canvas. I like the rough bumps on the surface of the fabric without all of the business of a printed pattern. To lessen the sparseness resulting from a lack of print, I use acrylic paint to stamp letters, words, or images onto the fabric. You can stamp on printed fabric, too, and can even go as far as using stamps to make a totally new fabric design rather than just printing a title or monogram.

### Play

Adhere a piece of canvas to a cardstock background. Distress the edges of a text block and a photograph with ink (see "How to Distress with Ink" on page 15), and adhere both to the page. Stamp a title with acrylic paint. Zigzag stitch around all edges of the canvas and randomly on the edges of the photograph. Straight stitch around the edges of the cardstock.

## Tabs

There are so many fun tabs available on the market today that have special sayings and cool patterns. I had my company logo made into a woven label. I normally use them for my quilts, but I have had fun using them as tabs in a couple of paper projects such as my moving card (see "Change of a Dress" on page 28) and a page about me (see "Me" on page 10). They're great for personalizing a project.

Smiles and a parade.

The day was bright and sunny. All of the teachers, the students and even some of the parents were decked out in their terrific Halloween finery. You could feel the excitement in the air as the kindergarten class led the entire school into town. Emily and Jane were adorable cheerleaders and they had lots of fun conversation along the parade route. There were lots of great costumes, happy smiles and fun memories on that beautiful fall day.

Clinton, New Jersey
October 2006

### Smile

Print journaling onto acetate and attach to a piece of cardstock with brads. Adhere tabs to a photograph and position photo corners around the photograph. Adhere the photograph to the cardstock and then adhere the cardstock to a background cardstock. Machine stitch around the edges of the main cardstock through both layers. Adhere a metal flower charm to the layout.

# Flowers

Flowers are so pretty on your scrapbooking pages. Use a premade flower (see "Sweet Sachet" on page 41) or make your own (see "Blue" on page 23). I also consider yo-yos to be a floral decoration in a fun and whimsical way.

## Niece

Make a pieced square by sewing strips of paper together with zigzag stitches. Round the corners with a corner rounding punch tool. Adhere the pieced paper to a background cardstock and zigzag around the edges. Add journaling to the page. Make three fabric yo-yos. Adhere a photograph, woven alphabet stickers, and the yo-yos to the layout.

## Masking

Masking is so much fun to do. I use it for titles, so I can make the lettering large for more impact. You can stencil or spray-paint the title. If using spray paint, remember to do it in a well-ventilated area.

### HOW TO MAKE A MASKED TITLE

1. Make letter templates from cardboard or template plastic and layer over the fabric.
2. Paint over the templates, remove the templates, and let dry.

### HOW TO MAKE A YO-YO FLOWER

1. Cut a 4" circle from fabric.
2. Turn ¼" of the outer edge to the wrong side and hand sew using a running stitch and a double length of thread.
3. Pull the thread tightly to gather up the fabric. Tie the thread ends in a knot and trim the tails.

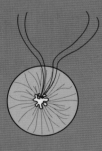

### Beach

Adhere fabric paper and a photograph to a cardstock background. Using cardstock letters as templates, mask a piece of canvas, spray with silver paint, and let dry. Stitch the canvas to the layout. Stitch around some edges of the cardstock and around the exposed edges of the fabric paper. Add journaling.

# EMBELLISHMENTS

Embellishments add that special finishing touch to a project or scrapbooking page. Try using beads, buttons, sequins, and other fabric notions, such as zippers, to get creative. Let your imagination take over.

## Beads

Small beads work well on paper projects. When using larger beads, look for beads that are relatively flat.

## Happily Ever After

Adhere a photograph to a piece of cardstock and trim to create a border. Trim one corner with scalloped scissors. Add journaling. Adhere the photograph to a cardstock background. Adhere a ribbon, flower, and woven label to the page. Glue a crystal in the center of the flower. Sew beads to the cardstock.

## Covered Buttons

You can use purchased fabric buttons to add some dimension to your projects. The buttons are available in many shapes and sizes. Alternatively, you can make your own fabric-covered button embellishments by using a button-making kit. These buttons, however, have a little more bulk to them.

### Faces of You

Cut five squares of patterned paper freehand and distress the edges with ink (see "How to Distress with Ink" on page 15). Adhere the patterned paper squares to a cardstock background. Sew a random grid pattern over the cardstock and patterned paper using both straight and zigzag stitches. Add edge stitching to the corners of some of the patterned squares. Adhere nine photographs to the page. Sew buttons and a transparency title to the page. Distress the edges of the cardstock with the edges of your scissors.

## Zippers
Add a little zing with zippers. They're great as design elements to break up a page, and you can use them opened or closed.

## John
Adhere a piece of cardstock and patterned paper to a cardstock background. Adhere a photograph, a journaling block, a zipper, and canvas alphabet stickers to the layout. Stitch around some edges of the cardstock and the patterned paper.

Our neighbor and friend, John, is a great guy! He adores the kids and loves to play with them. Adam and Alex ring his doorbell all of the time to try and entice him to come out and play. We're lucky to have him near us especially since our own families live in Canada. We call John our honorary Canadian and part of our family.

September 2006

# Embroidered Appliqués

The easiest way to make a classic and simple card is to purchase a package of embroidered appliqués from your local craft store and adhere them to cardstock. Some of the appliqués meant for scrapbooking have adhesive backs.

## It's a Boy

Adhere an embroidered sticker to a piece of cardstock and trim close to the edges of the sticker with pinking shears. Adhere the bordered design to the front of a blank card.

## Woven Labels

Adding a woven label to a project can dress up a simple page. Labels are available with alphabet letters as well as words and phrases.

### Grandmother

Print text onto a piece of card-stock. Round one corner of the photograph with a corner rounding punch tool. Adhere the photograph and a woven label to the cardstock and stitch along the bottom of the photograph. Add the date.

Aug '06

GRANDMOTHER

pure and simple love.

it's a beautiful thing.

Grandmother Irene and Ethan
Pembroke, Ontario Canada
2006

# Crochet

Crochet embellishments can add a lot of fun to your projects. Use booties for baby cards. Try doilies as backgrounds for vintage or romantic projects.

## Oh Boy!

Fold a piece of cardstock in half and trim to the desired card size. Adhere another piece of cardstock cut slightly smaller than the card to the card front. Punch a hole at each corner. Cut ribbon a few inches longer than each side of the card and insert the ends through the corner holes, taping them to the inside of the card. Clip a pair of crocheted booties together and adhere to the card. Adhere a woven label.

## Crystals

Add some sparkle to your projects with crystals. They come in a variety of colors and sizes and make great accents in the centers of flowers.

## Racquel

Adhere a photograph to a cardstock background. Machine stitch a couple of rows of stitching around the page. Partially stitch around the photo. Adhere a paper tab, a metal alphabet tile, clear flowers, and crystals to the layout. Add journaling.

## Sequins

Sequins can add subtle sheen and color to a project or can be used to create a polka-dot effect.

## Alex

Adhere fabric tabs to a photograph and adhere the photograph to a cardstock background. Adhere a piece of patterned paper and a journaling block to the cardstock and attach a ribbon, sequins, and a sticker. Zigzag stitch randomly around the edges of the photograph.

# BORDERS

Create borders on scrapbook pages with strips
of fabric or ribbons or with stamped images.

## Beach Babe

Adhere a piece of patterned paper and fabric border stickers to a cardstock background. Stitch around the edges of the
patterned paper. Make and attach a fabric border to the page. Adhere flowers to the layout and attach crystal brads at
the centers. Adhere a patterned envelope to the layout and zigzag stitch along each long side. Adhere two photographs
to cardstock and trim to create borders. Adhere the bordered photographs and alphabet stickers to the page.

# Fabric Borders

Fabric borders are a really simple way to dress up your pages with minimal fuss.

## HOW TO MAKE FABRIC BORDERS

1. Tear a strip of fabric 2" longer than the length or width of the paper.
2. Stretch the fabric across the paper, securing the ends on the reverse side.
3. Stitch the fabric in place.

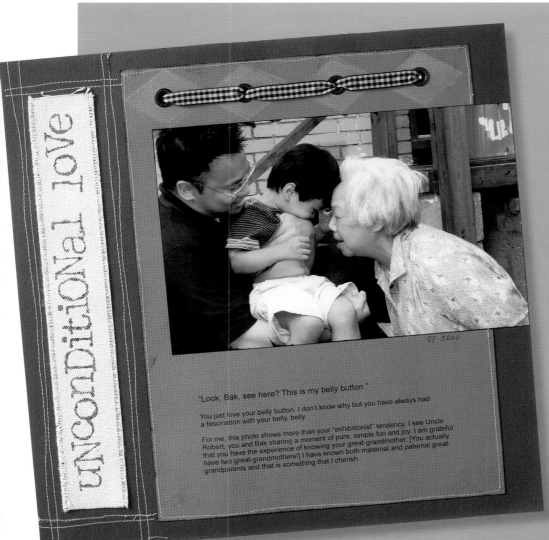

## Unconditional Love

Print text onto textured paper and distress the edges of the paper and a photograph with ink. Adhere the paper to a cardstock background. Adhere a purchased canvas border or make your own and adhere it to the background. Machine stitch around the border and around the edges of the textured paper. Stamp a border on the top edge of the textured paper with stamp pad ink. Punch holes along the top border, attach rivets, and tie ribbons through the holes. Distress the edges of the photograph with ink (see "How to Distress with Ink" on page 15), and adhere the photograph to the layout.

uNConDitioNaL loVe

"Look, Bak, see here? This is my belly button."

You just love your belly button. I don't know why but you have always had a fascination with your belly, belly.

For me, this photo shows more than your "exhibitionist" tendency. I see Uncle Robert, you and Bak sharing a moment of pure, simple fun and joy. I am grateful that you have the experience of knowing your great-grandmother. [You actually have two great-grandmothers!] I have known both maternal and paternal great-grandparents and that is something that I cherish.

## Stamped Fabric Borders

You can purchase or make your own stamped borders. It is an inexpensive way to add a little texture to your layout.

## HOW TO STAMP FABRIC BORDERS

1. Cut a strip of fabric to the desired size.
2. Stamp the fabric strip with rubber stamps and acrylic paint or stamp pad inks and let dry.

## Stitched Borders

Add hand embroidery stitches or buttons to fabric and ribbon borders to create borders with dimension. When adding a stitched border to a layout, be sure that any heavy items, such as buttons, are well adhered.

**Digging**

This is our favourite summer pastime. The bigger the sandpit the better. We take our shovels and pails everywhere we go and we stop at every park with a sandpit along the way. Then we pile back into the car wearing tons of dirt but that's ok because boys will be boys.

**Field of Dreams Park
Clinton, NJ**

**May 2005**

### Boys Will Be Boys

Sew buttons to a ribbon and secure one end of the ribbon to a garter buckle. Adhere the ribbon border to a cardstock background. Distress the edges of a photograph with ink (see "How to Distress with Ink" on page 15), and add journaling to the photo. Adhere a piece of fabric paper, the photograph, and a woven label to the cardstock background. Iron fusible alphabet letters to the layout and attach a transparent text block with brads.

# POCKETS AND ENVELOPES

Pockets and envelopes are fun additions to your project. They're great for hiding snippets of information when you want to keep the page visually clean.

## A Basic Envelope

Cut a piece of cardstock to 4¾" × 12" and fold in half, wrong sides together, to make a piece measuring 4¾" × 6". Punch curves at the corners using a corner rounder punch tool. Stitch ⅛" from both side edges to create an envelope. Punch a half circle in the center of the open edge using a circle punch.

## Paper Envelope

Use a paper envelope to hold a tag with journaling, additional photos, or memorabilia such as ticket stubs that don't coordinate with your layout. The envelope can be made from paper that coordinates with the other elements on the page.

## Taylor

Rubber stamp a flower image randomly across a piece of cardstock. Free-motion stitch around the stamped images (see "How to Free-Motion Stitch" on page 12) and edgestitch around the cardstock. Distress the edges of the cardstock with ink (see "How to Distress with Ink" on page 15). Adhere a photograph to cardstock and trim to create a border. Adhere the bordered photograph and alphabet stickers to the stamped cardstock. Attach a ribbon across the layout and attach a piece of ribbon across the corner of the photograph with brads. Adhere a recycled denim pocket and a flower to the layout. Make a tag and insert it into the pocket.

## Recycled Pockets

Recycled pockets, such as those found on denim
jackets, make great additions to scrapbook layouts.
They are perfect for inserting journaling notes.

## Wool Felt Envelope

Wool felt envelopes are perfect for
gift giving. Create one to hold a
holiday greeting, gift certificate or
piece of jewelry. Project instructions
are provided on page 71.

## Sweet Memories Quilt

Make this adorable
miniquilt to show
off everyday special
moments. Alter the look
of the quilt by changing
the contents of the
vinyl pockets. Project
instructions are provided
on page 71.

# VINYL AND TRANSPARENCIES

Vinyl and transparencies are fun for creating see-through accents. Print journaling text onto transparencies or cut titles from preprinted transparencies. For fabric projects, cut squares from vinyl and stitch them to your project to create see-through pockets.

### A Is for Alex

Print journaling onto a transparency. Trace around a letter stencil to draw the letter *A* onto the transparency. Cut out and remove the letter. Layer the transparency over a cardstock background and machine stitch around the letter and around the edge of the transparency. Zigzag stitch around the background cardstock. Adhere a photograph to the layout, attaching metal photo corners at the corners. Add the date.

## Stitching on Vinyl and Transparencies

You can sew on vinyl or transparency materials in the same manner as sewing on fabric or paper. If you encounter skipped stitches, adjust the tension on your machine.

## Brothers

Print journaling onto a transparency and stitch the transparency to patterned paper. Adhere the patterned paper to a cardstock background. Distress the edges of the photograph, the patterned paper, and metal alphabet letters for the title with ink (see "How to Distress with Ink" on page 15). Adhere the photograph, metal alphabet letters, and an alphabet sticker to the layout. Add the date. Add edge stitching to opposite corners of the photograph.

## Vellum Envelopes

A translucent envelope is a clean, crisp element. You can decorate it with bold stitching and rub-ons. On an otherwise visually busy page, it can provide a place in the layout for the eye to rest.

## Grow with Me

Personalize a growth chart for a young child. You can mark important milestones and put photographs or souvenirs in the little pockets. This cute growth chart is sure to encourage the child to keep a close eye on his or her development. Project instructions are provided on page 71.

## Chinatown

Adhere a piece of patterned paper and three photographs to a cardstock background. Stitch around the patterned paper and around the cardstock. Sew an envelope from vellum, mount it on a piece of patterned paper, and attach it to the layout. Make a paper tag with journaling (see "How to Make a Paper Tag" on page 27) and insert it into the envelope. Add rub-ons to the envelope.

## Pockets

Pockets from transparencies are great fun. You can decorate the top surface and still have the contents of the pocket peek through for an added effect.

## Baby Firsts

Print a page title onto cardstock and titles for the pockets onto a transparency. Cut four squares from patterned paper for the pocket backgrounds. Round the corners of the squares and the page title with a corner rounding punch tool. Adhere a piece of cardstock, the pocket backgrounds, and the page title to a piece of fabric paper. Cut four pockets from the printed transparency, layer over the pocket backgrounds, and stitch around three edges. Cut four pieces of patterned paper to fit into the transparency pockets, adhere fabric tabs and alphabet tabs to the papers, and insert them into the pockets. Attach a decorative brad to the center of the layout. Add journaling or photos to the reverse sides of the pocket inserts.

# PROJECT INSTRUCTIONS

## Ho Ho Ho Holiday Patchwork Pillow

Page 20

**Finished size:** 11½" × 12½"

### MATERIALS

1 fat quarter of red print for the top and back of the pillow
2 inkjet fabric sheets
1 woven label
Polyester fiberfill
Thread

### CUTTING

**From the red print, cut:**

3 rectangles, 3½" × 5¼"
1 rectangle, 4¼" × 13"
1 rectangle, 12" × 13"

### MAKING THE PILLOW

1. Print the photograph and text blocks onto the inkjet fabric sheet. Trim the photograph to 5¼" × 5¼", one text block to 5¼" × 5¼", and the other text block to 3½" × 3½".

2. Sew each of the photo and text blocks to a 3½" × 5¼" rectangle as shown to make three rows. Sew the rows together.

3. Sew the 4¼" × 13" rectangle to the right side of the pieced unit from step 2.

4. Pin the pillow front to the pillow back, right sides together. Stitch ¼" from the raw edges, leaving an opening for turning. Turn the pillow cover right side out and stuff with fiberfill. Hand stitch the opening closed.

## Bloom Wall Hanging

Page 25

**Finished size:** 14½" × 19½"

### MATERIALS

*All yardages are based on 42"-wide fabric.*

1 fat quarter of yellow print for the appliqué background

1 fat quarter *total* of 2 different blue prints for the piecing and appliqués

1 fat quarter *total* of 2 different fuchsia prints for the appliqués

1 fat quarter of pink print for the appliqué background

1 fat quarter *total* of 2 different lime green prints for the appliqués and the appliqué background

2 inkjet fabric sheets

15" × 20" rectangle of fabric for the backing

15" × 20" rectangle of batting

Fusible web

Stabilizer

## CUTTING

**From the yellow print fabric, cut:**

1 rectangle, 5" × 15"

**From the blue print fabric, cut:**

1 rectangle, 3¾" × 6½"

1 rectangle, 3" × 5"

**From the lime green print fabric, cut:**

1 rectangle, 5" × 12½"

**From the pink print fabric, cut:**

1 rectangle, 5" × 15"

## MAKING THE WALL HANGING

1. Prepare the appliqués and fuse them to the yellow, lime green, and pink print background fabrics, following "How to Make Fusible Fabric Appliqués" on page 23 and using the patterns on page 77. Sew a zigzag stitch around the appliqué pieces.

2. Print three photographs, each 4¼" × 6½" (size includes ¼" seam allowances). Stitch the three photographs and the 3¾" × 6½" blue print rectangle together to make row 2 as shown in the project photo on page 25.

3. Sew the 3" × 5" blue print rectangle to the right side of the lime green print rectangle to make row 3. Sew the rows together as shown in the project photo.

4. Baste the batting to the wrong side of the pieced top.

5. Pin the top to the backing fabric, right sides together. Sew ¼" from the raw edges, leaving a 3" opening for turning.

6. Turn the wall hanging right side out and hand stitch the opening closed. Quilt as desired.

# Keepsake Shoe Bag

Page 32

**Finished size:** Varies; custom-sized to fit shoes

## MATERIALS

1 inkjet iron-on transfer paper

Fabric for bag (amount depends on shoe size)

Ribbon, ⅛" wide

## MAKING THE SHOE BAG

1. Print the image onto the iron-on transfer sheet following the manufacturer's directions and referring to page 32. Trim to size.

2. Set the shoes together. Measure the pair of shoes and add extra for ease to determine the finished width and length of the shoe bag. Add a ¼" seam allowance to the side and bottom edges and a 2" hem allowance to the top. Cut two rectangles from fabric to these measurements.

3. Fuse the transfer image to one of the fabric rectangles, following the manufacturer's directions.

4. Pin the rectangles right sides together and, using a ¼" seam allowance, stitch the side and bottom edges. Fold ⅜" of the top edge to the wrong side, and then fold 1⅝". Stitch close to the first

fold all around. Stitch again ⅜" away to form the casing.

5. Turn the bag right side out. Along the sides of the bag front, snip through the outer fabric only, between the stitching lines, to create openings for the ties. Repeat on the bag back. Cut one length of ribbon to twice the width of the bag plus 18". Thread the ribbon through the casing, entering and exiting through the slits. Pull on the ribbon at one or both sides to gather the top. Tie the ribbon ends together at the side of the bag.

# Bébé You're Mine Wall Hanging

Page 34

**Finished size:** About 5½" × 5½", plus hanging loop; size varies depending on size of jeans used.

## MATERIALS

Pair of old jeans

Scrap of wool felt

2 crystals

⅓ yard of ribbon

Polyester fiberfill

Glue

## MAKING THE WALL HANGING

1. Cut off the lower portion of one blue jean leg so it is roughly square in shape. For this project, the lower portion of a pair of girl's blue jeans, including the ruffled hem, is 5½" x 5½".

2. Cut out the letters "bébé" and "BABY" from wool felt, using the patterns on page 79. Glue "bébé" to one side of the blue jeans piece. Glue "BABY" to the other side. Glue the crystals in place as shown or as desired.

3. Turn the piece inside out, right sides together, and align the cut edges. Insert the ends of a length of ribbon between the layers, even with the cut edges. Stitch ¼" from the edge, enclosing the ribbon ends in the seam.

4. Turn the piece right sides out, stuff with polyester fiberfill, and stitch closed across the bottom.

~~~

## Name Pillow

Page 35

**Finished size:** Varies; custom-sized to fit name appliqué

## MATERIALS

Fabric for the pillow front and back (amount depends on size of name appliqué)

Fabric for the appliqué letters

Fusible web

Polyester fiberfill

Stabilizer

## MAKING THE PILLOW

1. To make the letter templates, draw your own letters or type them on a computer in the desired font and size and print them onto paper. Cut out the individual letters.

2. Arrange the letter templates on a flat work surface to determine the finished length and width of the appliqué background. Add ¼" to all sides for the seam allowances. Cut two rectangles from fabric to these measurements for the pillow front and back.

3. Use the letter templates in reverse to prepare the letter appliqués, following "How to Make Fusible Fabric Appliqués" on page 23. Fuse the appliqués to the pillow front. Sew a tight zigzag stitch around the edges of the appliqués.

4. Pin the pillow front to the pillow back, right sides together. Stitch ¼" from the raw edges, leaving an opening for turning. Turn the pillow cover right side out and stuff with fiberfill. Hand stitch the opening closed.

~~~

## Initial Frieze

Page 35

**Finished size:** Varies; depends on the size of the canvas

## MATERIALS

Canvas for the background

Fabric for the initial

Fusible web

Acrylic craft paint in background color

Paintbrush

## MAKING THE FRIEZE

1. Type the initial on a computer in the desired font and size and print it onto paper. Cut out the letter to make a template.

2. Use the letter template in reverse to prepare the initial appliqué, following "How to Make Fusible Fabric Appliqués" on page 23.

3. Paint the canvas in a coordinating color and let dry. Fuse the letter to the front of the canvas, following the manufacturer's directions.

~~~

## Sweet Sachet

Page 41

**Finished size:** 3" × 4"

## MATERIALS

Two 3½" × 4½" rectangles of fabric for the front and back

Several 5" lengths of ribbon in a variety of styles

1 fabric flower

1 crystal

Fusible web

Dried lavender flowers for sachet filling

## MAKING THE SACHET

1. Apply fusible web to the right side of each fabric rectangle, following the manufacturer's directions.

2. Remove the paper backing from one rectangle. Layer ribbons edge to edge on the rectangle and fuse in place. Zigzag stitch along the edges of the ribbons. Repeat for the second rectangle.

3. Pin the two rectangles right sides together and stitch ¼" from the edges, leaving an opening on one edge for turning.

4. Turn the sachet cover right side out and fill with lavender.

5. Hand stitch the opening closed. Adhere the flower and crystal.

# Wool Felt Envelope

Page 63

**Finished size:** 5⅜" × 2¾"

## MATERIALS

8½" × 11" piece of wool felt

Woven label

Scrap of fusible web

## MAKING THE ENVELOPE

1. Cut one 5⅜" × 2¾" rectangle from wool felt for the envelope back. Cut one top flap, one bottom, and two side pieces from wool felt, using the patterns on page 79.

2. Layer the side pieces over the bottom piece, aligning the edges at the corners. Stitch along the diagonal edges through both

layers. Layer the unit over the envelope back, aligning the edges, and edgestitch around three sides. Layer the top flap over the pieced unit and edgestitch across the top edge.

3. Fuse a woven label to the envelope flap.

# Sweet Memories Quilt

Page 63

Finished size: 9" × 9"

## MATERIALS

12" square of orange print for the blocks

12" square of yellow print for the blocks

1 fat quarter of fuchsia print for the blocks and backing

12" square of vinyl for the pockets

9½" × 9½" square of batting

Rub-on letters

8" length of ribbon

2 clips

## CUTTING

**From the orange print, cut:**
3 squares, 3½" × 3½"

**From the yellow print, cut:**
3 squares, 3½" × 3½"

**From the fuchsia print, cut:**
3 squares, 3½" × 3½"
1 square, 9½" × 9½"

**From the vinyl, cut:**
4 squares, 3" × 3"

## MAKING THE QUILT

1. Sew three print squares together in a row. Repeat to make three rows. Stitch the rows together to make the quilt top as shown at left.

2. Layer the quilt top and the backing right sides together, lay the batting on top, and pin. Stitch ¼" from the outer edges through all the layers, leaving a 3" opening for turning. Turn right side out and hand stitch the opening closed.

3. Layer the vinyl squares over some of the quilt squares and stitch around the side and bottom edges to create pockets.

4. Add rub-ons to the vinyl pockets. Attach the clips to the top edge of the quilt and tie the ribbon through the clips for a hanger.

# Grow with Me

Page 66

**Finished size:** 8" × 36½"

## MATERIALS

9" × 37½" rectangle of canvas

1 fat quarter each of 4 or 5 different fabrics for the pockets and measurement markers

8" × 10" piece of vinyl for pocket covers

⅜ yard of fusible web, 18" wide

2 large decorative grommets

10" length of ribbon

Alphabet rubber stamps

Acrylic paint

## CUTTING

**From the fat quarters, cut:**
30 rectangles (total), 1" × 3"
4 rectangles (total), 3¼" × 3¾"

**From the vinyl, cut:**
4 rectangles, 3¼" x 3¾"

## MAKING THE GROWTH CHART

1. Fold both long edges of the canvas ½" to the wrong side and stitch ¼" from the edges. Repeat on the top and bottom edges.

2. Apply fusible web to the back of the 1" × 3" rectangles, following the manufacturer's directions. Fuse the rectangles to the canvas, creating a vertical column on the left side.

3. Apply fusible web to wrong side of the 3¼" × 3¾" rectangles and fuse to the right side of the canvas. Align the vinyl rectangles on the fused rectangles and edgestitch around the side and bottom edges.

4. Rubber stamp the name at the top of the canvas using acrylic paint and let dry. Attach the grommets, thread a ribbon end through each grommet, and stitch to secure.

# PRODUCT CREDITS

## ME

Page 10

**Alphabet letters** Scrapworks **Flower** Heidi Swapp and Making Memories **Metal Tab** Autumn Leaves **Woven label** www.clothing4u.com

## SUMMER FUN

Page 11

**Alphabet stickers** Pressed Petals **Cardstock** KI Memories **Flower** Prima Marketing **Patterned paper** Anna Griffin

## THANK YOU

Page 12

**Cardstock** KI Memories **Crystals** Heidi Swapp **Woven label** Me and My Big Ideas **Rubber Stamp** Autumn Leaves

## LOVE U

Page 12

**Acrylic paint and Chipboard alphabet letter** Making Memories **Cardstock** Bazzill Basics Paper **Patterned paper** Chatterbox **Photo Turn** 7 Gypsies

## EMILY AT 4

Page 13

**Alphabet sticker** Me and My Big Ideas **Cardstock** Bazzill Basics Paper **Patterned paper** Anna Griffin **Ribbon** KI Memories

## COOL

Page 13

**Acrylic embellishments, Cardstock and Patterned paper** KI Memories **Rub-on** Making Memories

## HOPE

Page 14

**Alphabet stickers** EK Success **Brad** Making Memories **Cardstock** Bazzill Basics Paper **Fabric** Moda Fabrics **Fabric embellishment** EK Success

## FIRST RIDE

Page 16

**Cardstock** The Paper Company **Embroidery floss** DMC **Ribbons and Rub-ons** Making Memories

## SNOW

Page 16

**Alphabet letters** Basic Grey **Cardstock** Bazzill Basics Paper **Fabric paper** Michael Miller Memories **Snowflakes** Heidi Swapp

## RAIN
Page 17

**Alphabet stickers** Li'l Davis Designs **Cardstock and Patterned paper** KI Memories **Thread** YLI

## DANIEL
Page 18

**Cardstock** Bazzill Basics Paper **Chipboard alphabet stickers** Making Memories **Patterned paper** Basic Grey **Photo turn** 7 Gypsies **Ribbon** Making Memories

## FRIEND
Page 19

**Alphabet stickers** Making Memories **Cardstock** Bazzill Basics Paper **Patterned paper** 7 Gypsies and Pebbles

## HO HO HO HOLIDAY PATCHWORK PILLOW
Page 20

**Inkjet fabric sheet** Printed Treasures by Milliken **Woven label** Me and My Big Ideas

## LOVE

Page 21

**Alphabet letters** Making Memories **Brads** EK Success **Cardstock** Bazzill Basics Paper and KI Memories **Fabric** Anna Griffin (Windham Fabrics) **Fabric Embellishment** EK Success

## H
Page 22

**Cardstock** KI Memories **Cardstock letter** *h* (used as a template) Basic Grey **Patterned paper** Chatterbox

## LITTLE PINK PURSE CARD
Page 23

**Cardstock** Bazzill Basics Paper **Fabric paper** Michael Miller

## BLUE
Page 23

**Cardstock** Bazzill Basics Paper and KI Memories **Crystals** Heidi Swapp

## INDEPENDENCE
Page 23

**Cardstock** Bazzill Basics Paper **Fabric** Marcus Brothers Textiles **Fusible web (Steam-A-Seam 2)** The Warm Company

## VROOM

Page 24

**Alphabet sticker** Li'l Davis Designs **Cardstock** Bazzill Basics Paper **Fabric tabs** Scrapworks **Patterned paper** KI Memories

## BLOOM WALL HANGING
Page 25

**Fusible web (Steam-A-Seam 2)** The Warm Company **Inkjet fabric sheets** Printed Treasures by Milliken

## PAPER TAG
Page 27

**Cardstock** Bazzill Basics Paper **Patterned paper** My Mind's Eye **Ribbon** SEI

## HUGS
Page 27

**Alphabet stickers** Li'l Davis Designs **Brad** Foofala **Cardstock** Bazzill Basics Paper **Patterned paper** Chatterbox and 7 Gypsies **Ribbon** SEI

## CHANGE OF A DRESS
Page 28

**Cardstock** Bazzill Basics Paper **Fabric** Moda Fabrics **Woven label** clothinglabels4u.com

## FABRIC TAG
Page 28

**Fabric** Free Spirit Fabric **Ribbon** SEI **Stabilizer** Pellon

## BABY TAG
Page 28

**Alphabet stickers** EK Success **Cardstock** Bazzill Basics Paper **Inkjet fabric sheet** Printed Treasures by Milliken **Ribbon** SEI

## GET CLOSER
Page 29

**Alphabet stickers** Chatterbox **Brads** Making Memories **Cardstock** Bazzill Basics Paper **Chipboard alphabet letter** Li'l Davis Designs **Flowers** Prima Marketing **Patterned paper** Paper Adventures **Ribbon** Making Memories

### ALEX SWEET BABY

Page 30

**Cardstock** Bazzill Basics Paper **Inkjet fabric sheet** Printed Treasures by Milliken **Patterned paper and ribbon** Making Memories

### HOLIDAY ORNAMENT

Page 31

**Cardstock** Bazzill Basics Paper **Inkjet fabric sheet** Printed Treasures by Milliken **Ribbon** KI Memories

### MIRACLE

Page 31

**Alphabet stickers** Li'l Davis Designs **Cardstock** Bazzill Basics Paper **Chipboard frame** Li'l Davis Designs **Inkjet fabric sheet** Printed Treasures by Milliken **Labels** Dymo **Patterned paper** KI Memories **Ribbon** Making Memories

### KEEPSAKE SHOE BAG

Page 32

**Iron-on transfer paper** Printed Treasures by Milliken **Narrow ribbon** Making Memories

### JACK

Page 33

**Inkjet fabric sheet** Printed Treasures by Milliken

### BÉBÉ YOU'RE MINE WALL HANGING

Page 34

**Ribbon** Mokuba

### NAME PILLOW

Page 35

**Fabric** Free Spirit Fabric **Fusible web (Steam-A-Seam 2)** The Warm Company

### INITIAL FRIEZE

Page 35

**Fabric** Moda Fabrics **Fusible web (Steam-A-Seam 2)** The Warm Company

### LOVE GREETING CARD

Page 36

**Flower** Prima Marketing **Ribbon** Making Memories

### FISHING

Page 36

**Alphabet stickers** Making Memories **Cardstock** Bazzill Basics Paper **Fabric letters** Li'l Davis Designs **Fabric paper** Me and My Big Ideas **Rub-ons** Making Memories

### BE MERRY

Page 37

**Cardstock** Bazzill Basics Paper **Patterned** paper 7 Gypsies **Ribbon** Making Memories

### L

Page 38

**Letter** Pottery Barn Kids **Ribbon** Autumn Leaves

### BROTHER AND SISTER

Page 38

**Buttons** EK Success **Cardstock** Bazzill Basics Paper **Grommets and Ribbon** Making Memories **Patterned paper** Chatterbox

### SWEET

Page 39

**Acrylic letter tiles** Doodlebug Designs **Brads** Chatterbox **Cardstock and Patterned paper** KI Memories **Flowers** Making Memories **Plastic sleeve** Karen Foster Design **Ribbon** American Crafts **Rub-on** Scrapworks

### SUPER STAR

Page 40

**Cardstock** Bazzill Basics Paper **Fabric sticker and ribbon** Making Memories **Metal clip** Advantus **Patterned paper** KI Memories

### ALYSSA

Page 40

**Alphabet stickers** Making Memories **Photo corners** Heidi Swapp

**EMILY'S HOLIDAY**
Page 41

**Acrylic paint** Plaid Enterprises
**Cardstock** Bazzill Basics Paper
**Chipboard alphabet letter and Ribbons**
Making Memories **Linen** Charles Craft
**Patterned paper** Basic Grey and 7
Gypsies

**SWEET SACHET**
Page 41

**Flower** Prima Marketing **Ribbons**
American Crafts **Fusible web (Steam-
A-Seam 2)** The Warm Company

**E**
Page 42

**Alphabet sticker** Li'l Davis Designs
**Bleach pen** Clorox **Cardstock** KI
Memories **Crystals and Rubber stamp**
Heidi Swapp

**FALL**

Page 43

**Cardstock** Bazzill Basics Paper **Fabric**
Free Spirit Fabric **Patterned paper**
Sweetwater **Rubber stamps** Heidi
Swapp

**FOLLOW YOUR DREAMS**
Page 44

**Cardstock** The Paper Company **Inkjet
fabric sheets** Printed Treasures by
Milliken **Woven label** Me and My Big
Ideas

**EXPLORE**
Page 45

**Cardstock** Bazzill Basics Paper **Inkjet
fabric sheet** Printed Treasures by
Milliken **Rub-ons** Making Memories

**INTENSE**
Page 46

**Alphabet stickers** 7 Gypsies **Cardstock**
Bazzill Basics Paper **Fabric paper** Me
and My Big Ideas

**NEW TRADITIONS**
Page 47

**Cardstock** Bazzill Basics Paper **Fabric**
Anna Griffin **Metal clip** 7 Gypsies
**Woven label** Me and My Big Ideas

**CURLY QS**
Page 48

**Brad, Fabric tab, and Metal letter**
Making Memories **Cardstock** Bazzill
Basics Paper **Fabric** Moda Fabrics
**Rubber stamps** Heidi Swapp

**PLAY**
Page 48

**Cardstock** KI Memories **Rubber stamps**
Heidi Swapp

**SMILE**

Page 49

**Cardstock** Bazzill Basics Paper **Metal
flower charm** Making Memories **Photo
corners** Heidi Swapp **Tabs** Scrapworks

**NIECE**
Page 50

**Alphabet stickers** Making Memories
**Cardstock and Patterned paper** KI
Memories

**BEACH**
Page 51

**Cardstock** KI Memories **Cardstock
alphabet letters** Basic Grey **Paint**
Simply Spray

**HAPPILY EVER AFTER**
Page 52

**Beads** Matsuno **Flower** Prima
Marketing **Woven label** Making
Memories

**FACES OF YOU**

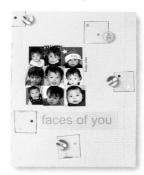

Page 53

**Buttons** Junkitz **Cardstock and
Patterned paper** KI Memories

**JOHN**
Page 54

**Canvas alphabet stickers** Li'l Davis
Designs **Cardstock** Bazzill Basics
Paper **Patterned paper** 7 Gypsies
**Zipper** Junkitz

**IT'S A BOY**
Page 55

**Cardstock** Bazzill Basics Paper
**Embroidery sticker** K and Company

## GRANDMOTHER

Page 55

**Cardstock** Bazzill Basics Paper **Woven label** Me and My Big Ideas

## OH BOY!

Page 56

**Cardstock** KI Memories **Ribbon** Doodlebug Designs **Woven label** Me and My Big Ideas

## RACQUEL

Page 00

**Cardstock** KI Memories **Crystals and Flowers** Heidi Swapp **Metal alphabet tile** Making Memories **Patterned paper** Chatterbox

## ALEX

Page 57

**Patterned paper** KI Memories **Fabric tabs** Scrapworks **Ribbon** American Crafts **Sequins** Hero Arts **Sticker** Crossed Paths

## BEACH BABE

Page 58

**Alphabet stickers, Cardstock and Patterned paper** KI Memories **Brads** Making Memories **Cardstock** Bazzill Basics Paper **Fabric Stickers** Mrs. Grossman's **Flowers** Making Memories

## UNCONDITIONAL LOVE

Page 59

**Cardstock** Bazzill Basics Paper **Canvas title** Li'l Davis Designs **Rivets** Chatterbox **Rubber stamp** Hero Arts

## BOYS WILL BE BOYS

Page 60

**Brads** Chatterbox **Buttons** Junkitz **Garter buckle** 7 Gypsies **Cardstock** Bazzill Basics Paper **Fabric paper** Me and My Big Ideas **Iron-on alphabet** Heidi Swapp **Woven label** Making Memories

## A BASIC ENVELOPE

Page 61

**Cardstock** Anna Griffin

## TAYLOR

Page 62

**Alphabet stickers** 7 Gypsies **Cardstock** The Paper Company **Ribbon** KI Memories **Rubber stamp** Hero Arts **Flower** Creative Co-Op

## WOOL FELT ENVELOPE

Page 63

**Woven label** Me and My Big Ideas

## SWEET MEMORIES QUILT

Page 63

**Fabric** Free Spirit Fabric **Rub-ons and Clips** Making Memories

## A IS FOR ALEX

Page 64

**Cardstock** KI Memories **Photo Corners** Daisy D's **Transparency** Avery

## BROTHERS

Page 65

**Alphabet sticker** Li'l Davis Designs **Patterned paper and Metal alphabet letters** KI Memories **Transparency** Avery

## CHINATOWN

Page 66

**Cardstock** Bazzill Basics Paper **Patterned paper** Chatterbox **Ribbon** American Crafts **Rub-ons** Autumn Leaves

## GROW WITH ME

Page 66

**Acrylic paint and Grommets** Making Memories **Fabric** Free Spirit **Fusible web (Steam-A-Seam 2)** The Warm Company **Rubber stamps** Heidi Swapp

## BABY FIRSTS

Page 67

**Fabric paper** Me and My Big Ideas **Fabric tabs** Making Memories **Patterned paper** My Mind's Eye **Woven alphabet tabs** Scrapworks

# PATTERNS

**Patterns for Bloom Wall Hanging**
Do not add seam allowances.
Patterns are reversed for fusible appliqué.

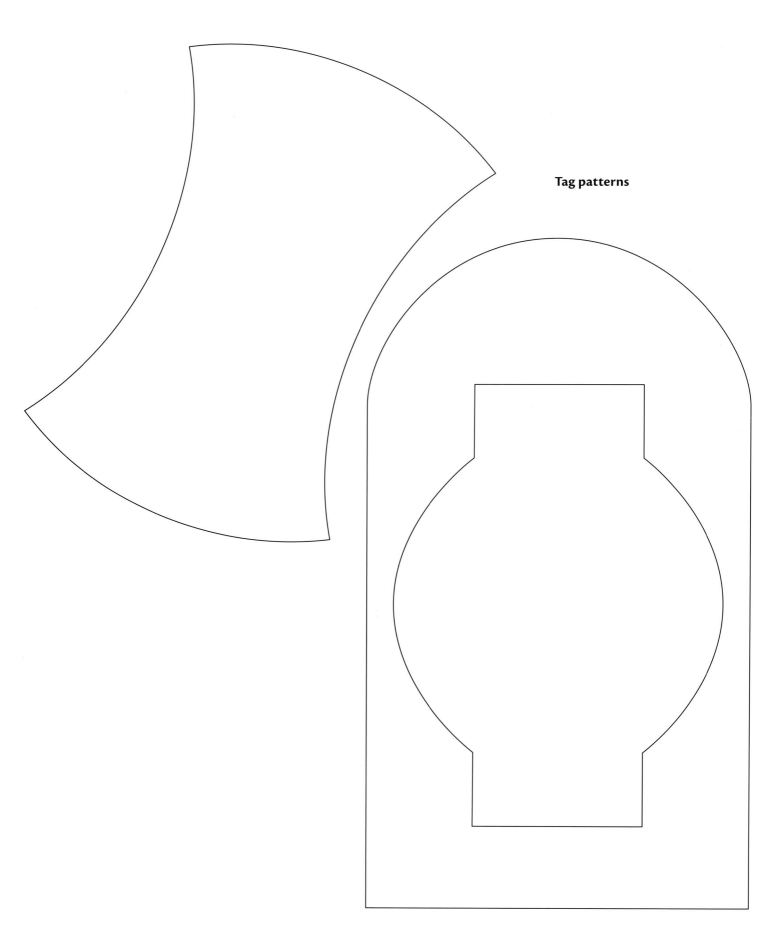

**Tag patterns**

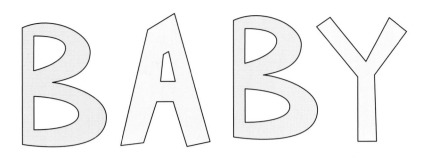

**Patterns for Bébé You're Mine Wall Hanging**
Do not add seam allowances.

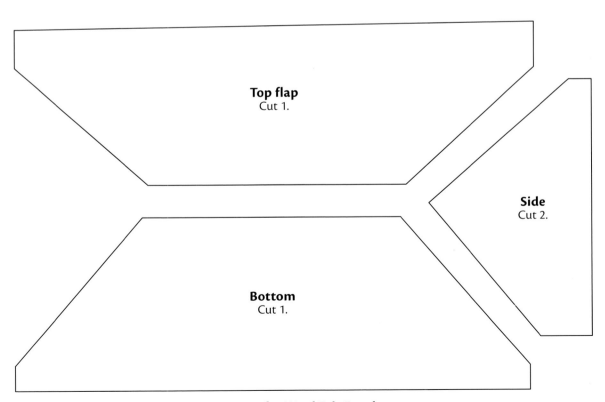

**Top flap**
Cut 1.

**Side**
Cut 2.

**Bottom**
Cut 1.

**Patterns for Wool Felt Envelope**
Do not add seam allowances.

# ABOUT THE AUTHOR

Linda Lum DeBono was born and raised in Canada. She's been a crafty girl all her life. She graduated from the University of Toronto with a degree in science and later worked in the pharmaceutical industry. At the same time, she started her first artsy venture, a greeting card company called The Paper Gallery.

After moving to New Jersey with her husband, Linda Lum DeBono taught herself how to quilt and soon she was designing. Her work has appeared in Better Homes and Gardens' *American Patchwork and Quilting*, its sister publication, *Quilts and More*, and Primedia's *Quilt It for Christmas*. She has appeared in *Quilter's Home* magazine as well.

After taking some time off, she is now back in full force. She is designing fabric for Henry Glass in New York City and has written several books.

Linda Lum DeBono lives in Clinton, New Jersey, with her fabulous and supportive husband, Reno, and her two wild and lovable kids, Adam and Alex.